Queen Elizabeth II and her family

DK

Penguin Random House

Editorial Abi Luscombe; Rona Skene
Design Eleanor Bates
Jacket Design Sonny Flynn
Special Sales and Custom Executive Issy Walsh
Picture Research Aditya Katyal
Production Editor Dragana Puvacic
Senior Production Controller Ena Matagic
Publisher Francesca Young
Deputy Art Director Mabel Chan
Publishing Director Sarah Larter

Material in this publication was previously
published in *The Queen and Her Family* (2016)

First American Edition, 2023
Published in the United States by DK Publishing
1745 Broadway, 20th Floor, New York, NY 10019

Copyright © 2023 Dorling Kindersley Limited
DK, a Division of Penguin Random House LLC
23 24 25 26 27 10 9 8 7 6 5 4 3 2 1
001–337023–Jan/2023

A catalog record for this book
is available from the Library of Congress.
ISBN: 978-0-7440-8594-5

Printed and bound in Slovakia

For the curious
www.dk.com

The publisher would like to thank the following for their kind
permission to reproduce their photographs:
(Key: a-above; b-below/bottom; c-centre; f-far; l-left; r-right; t-top)

akg-images: arkivi 9r; **Alamy Stock Photo:** Action Plus Sports Images 40cra, dpa picture alliance / Rolf Vennenbernd
38-39, / Royal Press Europe-A. Nieboer 40clb, Doug Peters / EMPICS 40crb, Granger, NYC 9tl, Barrie Harwood 47tr, PA
Images / Chris Jelf 56, robertharding / Rolf Richardson 37br, 41tc, United Archives GmbH / IFA Film 67tl, ViewFromAbove
10-11, World History Archive 7bl, Allan Wright 30; **Avalon:** EPN / Newscom 61; **Dreamstime.com:** Ilyach 74-75;
Getty Images: AFP / Fiona Hanson 45, / Dominic Lipinski 58, AFP / POOL / Dan Kitwood 70, / Joe Giddens 73, AFP Photo
/ Hugo Burnand / Clarence House 52-53, David M. Benett 41clb, Matt Cardy 60, Carl Court 26, 28, Central Press / Hulton
Archive 21, Corbis Historical / Ipsumpix 7cl, James Gill - Danehouse 48, De Agostini / DEA / G. Nimatallah 7tl, Elsa 41crb,
Fox Photos / Hulton Archive 20, Gamma-Rapho / Jean Guichard 67cra, Tim Graham 9bl, 16-17b, 32, Handout / The
Duchess of Cambridge 57, Hulton Fine Art Collection / Heritage Images 7cr, / Print Collector / Ann Ronan Pictures 7tr,
Lisa Sheridan / Studio Lisa / Hulton Archive 3tr, 13, Anwar Hussein 27tr, 55br, The Image Bank Unreleased / Gideon
Mendel 34-35, Indigo 36, 50, Max Mumby / Indigo 37t, 38cl, 40cb, 41cra, 47bl, Chris Jackson 40cla, 41cla, 41cb, 54, 55t,
Georges De Keerle 43, Keystone / Hulton Archive 31, Lichfield 35tr, Martin H. Simon-Pool 33, POOL / Tim Graham Picture
Library 18, Popperfoto 14-15, Terry Fincher / Princess Diana Archive 48cla, STAFF / AFP 63, Topical Press Agency / Hulton
Archive 12, Mark Cuthbert / UK Press 3br, 6, 46cra, Cecil Beaton / Underwood Archives 42, WPA Pool / Pool / Richard
Pohle 64-65, Karwai Tang / WireImage 51, WireImage / Anwar Hussein Collection / ROTA 29, Arthur Edwards - WPA Pool
24-25, Chris Jackson - WPA Pool 5, 41tl, Jonathan Brady - WPA Pool 46b, WPA Pool / Niall Carson 71;
Mary Evans Picture Library: Illustrated London News Ltd 3cr, 44; **Shutterstock.com:** 19, 40cb (Peter), Aaron Chown /
AP 1b, Design Pics Inc 8, Undated handout photo issued by Kensington Palace of Prince Louis ahead of his fourth
birthday on Saturday / Duchess of Cambridge / WPA Pool 59, Kerim Okten / EPA 62, Robin Utrecht 68; **SuperStock:**
Classic Vision / age fotostock 7br; **V&A Images / Victoria and Albert Museum, London:** © Cecil Beaton 23

Cover images: *Front:* **Getty Images:** Bettmann

All other images © Dorling Kindersley

MIX
Paper | Supporting
responsible forestry
FSC™ C018179

This book was made with Forest
Stewardship Council™ certified
paper – one small step in DK's
commitment to a sustainable future.
For more information go to
www.dk.com/our-green-pledge

Contents

Queen Elizabeth II

Her Majesty Queen Elizabeth II reigned for 70 years, making her the longest-reigning British monarch in history.

Like a queen in a fairy tale, Queen Elizabeth lived in palaces and castles. She even wore a crown. The British monarch has a selection of crowns to choose from, depending on the occasion.

Everyone who met Queen Elizabeth greeted her with a small curtsy or bow, or shook hands. If they were introduced to her, they called her "Your Majesty".

Kings and queens of Britain

For more than 1,500 years, kings and queens have reigned in Great Britain. The British throne is passed down through family lines, so most of those past monarchs were ancestors of Queen Elizabeth II.

Although the monarch is called the Head of State, the laws of Great Britain are made by Parliament, which is elected by the people of the nation. This system is known as a constitutional monarchy.

Queen Elizabeth II

Here are some past British monarchs:

King Henry VIII

Queen Elizabeth I

King George III

Queen Victoria

King Edward VII

King George VI

The Crown Jewels

The Crown Jewels are a collection of royal ceremonial objects, such as crowns, sceptres, and orbs. Many are priceless treasures, featuring the world's largest gems. The Crown Jewels are symbols of the British monarchy and are used for traditional ceremonies, including coronations and the annual State Opening of Parliament.

Since the 14th century, the Crown Jewels have been kept at the Tower of London, where they are guarded by the Yeoman Warders, also known as Beefeaters. Every year, millions of visitors see the Crown Jewels on public display.

The Sovereign's Orb is a gold sphere that is placed in the monarch's right hand during the coronation.

The Coronation Spoon and Ampulla are used during coronations. Holy oil is poured from the eagle-shaped Ampulla into the spoon.

The Sovereign's Sceptre with Cross is set with the Cullinan I diamond, one of the world's largest diamonds.

Queen Victoria's crown is a small diamond headdress that was made for her after the death of her husband, Prince Albert.

Windsor Castle

An official residence of the British Royal Family for more than 1,000 years, Windsor Castle sits on the banks of the River Thames at Windsor, a town just west of London. It stands in a

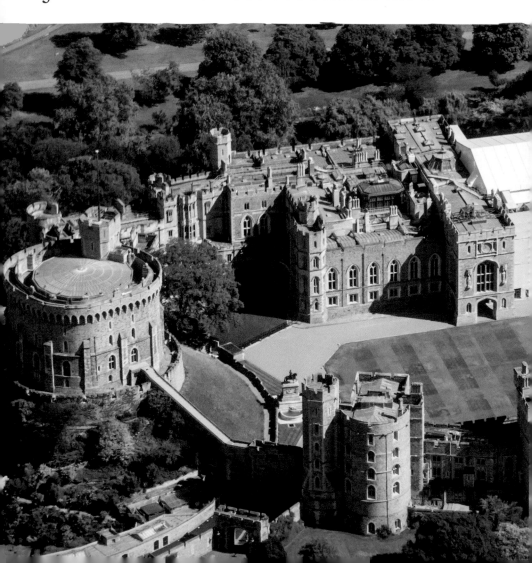

former royal hunting ground, which is now a large park where deer still roam. Queen Elizabeth often spent weekends at Windsor Castle and used it to host official visits by overseas leaders. Some of the castle and its grounds are open to the public.

An aerial view of Windsor Castle

Princess Elizabeth

Princess Elizabeth Alexandra Mary was born on 21 April 1926. Elizabeth and her sister, Margaret, spent their early childhood in a large house in London, where they had a governess to teach them. Elizabeth loved dogs and horses, a passion that lasted her whole life.

Elizabeth's life changed when her father became King George VI. The family moved to Buckingham Palace and the princesses became role models for the nation's children.

As the King's eldest daughter, Elizabeth knew that she would one day be queen.

Elizabeth (left) and Margaret (right) joined a Girl Guide company at Buckingham Palace.

Princess Elizabeth with two of her corgis in 1936. The corgi was her favourite breed of dog.

Coronation of King George VI
When Elizabeth's uncle, Edward VIII, decided he did not want to be king, Elizabeth's father took his place and became King George VI. This picture of the King and his family was taken on Coronation day in 1937. Next to King George is his mother, Queen Mary.

Buckingham Palace

The monarch's official London residence is Buckingham Palace. The Royal Standard flag flies from the roof of the palace when the monarch is at home. Of the palace's 775 rooms, the grandest are the State Rooms, used for official ceremonies and entertaining.

Buckingham Palace is the setting for grand displays of pageantry, such as the Changing the Guard ceremony, when the palace guards hand over to a new set of soldiers. The annual Trooping the Colour parade marks the official birthday of the monarch in June. The ceremony begins and ends at Buckingham Palace.

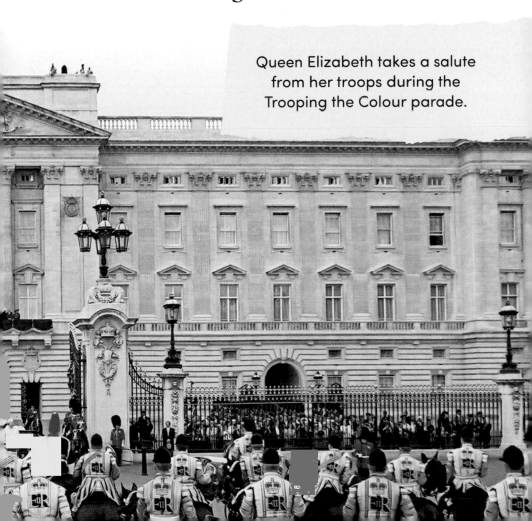

Queen Elizabeth takes a salute from her troops during the Trooping the Colour parade.

Inside the Palace

During Queen Elizabeth's reign, around 50,000 people a year were invited to garden parties, banquets, and receptions at Buckingham Palace. In 1993, Queen Elizabeth allowed parts of the palace to open to the public. Every summer, visitors can see state rooms such as the ornate ballroom and the Throne Room.

When the ballroom was built in 1856, it was the largest room in London.

The lavish Throne Room is used on formal occasions, such as coronations, jubilees, and royal weddings.

World War II

When World War II started in 1939, Elizabeth was 13 years old. London was the target of frequent bombing raids, but her parents, the King and Queen, remained at Buckingham Palace to show their support for the people of London. Elizabeth and Margaret moved to Windsor Castle, just outside London.

The King and Queen inspect bomb damage to Buckingham Palace in 1940.

The princesses wanted to help the war effort, too. The girls sewed and knitted clothing for the troops. They also broadcast on the radio to boost people's spirits. As soon as she was old enough, Elizabeth joined the Auxiliary Territorial Service (ATS), where she served as a driver and mechanic. World War II ended in 1945, when Elizabeth was 19.

By the end of World War II, Princess Elizabeth was a Junior Commander in the ATS.

The Coronation

When her father, King George VI, died in 1952, Princess Elizabeth inherited the throne. On 2 June 1953, she was officially crowned Queen Elizabeth II. Following tradition, the Coronation took place at Westminster Abbey in London. Thousands of people lined the streets, and millions more watched the event on television.

In her Coronation speech, the young Queen vowed, "Throughout all my life and with all my heart I shall strive to be worthy of your trust."

This photograph shows Queen Elizabeth II with the royal regalia from the Crown Jewels. Although she is wearing the Imperial State Crown, her official Coronation crown was the solid gold, jewel-encrusted St Edward's Crown.

Parliament

As Head of State, one of Queen Elizabeth's most important duties was the State Opening of Parliament, where she appeared in the royal regalia. MPs and members of the House of Lords gathered to hear the Queen read a speech outlining the government's plans for the following parliamentary session.

In her 70-year reign, Queen Elizabeth only missed this annual event three times – in 1959 and 1963 when she was expecting her children Andrew and Edward, and in 2022, the last year of her reign, when Prince Charles stood in for her.

When Queen Elizabeth opened parliament in 2015, she was accompanied by Prince Philip, Prince Charles, and the Duchess of Cornwall.

Meeting people

During her reign, Queen Elizabeth met hundreds of outstanding achievers from all walks of life.

One of the Queen's duties was to meet the prime minister weekly. In her reign, she met with 15 different prime ministers. She also welcomed many world leaders to Britain, including South African president Nelson Mandela.

A carriage ride in London with Nelson Mandela in 1996

Queen Elizabeth met US president Barack Obama several times. She even invited his daughters to Buckingham Palace and offered to drive them around in her gold carriage!

Queen Elizabeth also honoured the achievements of British people.

Barack and Michelle Obama with Queen Elizabeth in 2009

Famous broadcaster and campaigner David Attenborough received a knighthood for his work. Also, in 2021, Professor Sarah Gilbert received a damehood for helping to create vaccines to fight COVID-19.

Sir David Attenborough and Queen Elizabeth in 2019

Around Britain

Imagine if the monarch came to visit your school! Every year, members of the Royal Family attend about 3,000 public engagements around Britain.

Queen Elizabeth took part in thousands of official ceremonies. She travelled all over the country, visiting schools, hospitals, community centres, charities, and businesses.

Queen Elizabeth II lays a wreath during the annual Remembrance Sunday Service at the Cenotaph on Whitehall, London, in November 2015.

Queen Elizabeth looks at a collage made by children at
Southwark Cathedral, London, in December 2006.

Wherever she went, Queen Elizabeth
would be welcomed by bands and
choirs, and children would often present
her with posies of flowers. She enjoyed
meeting the people of Britain and
finding out about their lives.

Balmoral Castle

Of all her Royal residences, Balmoral Castle in Scotland was one of Queen Elizabeth's favourites. She loved the spectacular countryside surrounding the castle, and was a great fan of the Highland Games, held every year in the nearby village of Braemar.

As a girl, Princess Elizabeth and her sister Margaret would stay at Balmoral

View of Balmoral Castle in Royal Deeside, Scotland

all through the summer, where they had space and freedom to ride their horses and go on picnics in the vast grounds.

When she became Queen, Elizabeth continued the tradition, taking her children to Balmoral every summer. They enjoyed relaxing together, horseriding, and walking their dogs. At family barbecues, Prince Philip always took charge of the cooking! In later years, her grandchildren and great-granchildren loved their Balmoral summers, too.

Queen Elizabeth and her family at Balmoral in 1960

World traveller

The Queen was a popular international figure. She acted as an ambassador for the UK, promoting its image and helping to form friendly relationships with other countries.

During her reign, she travelled widely. Her first official trip was a tour of the Commonwealth, a group of countries with links to the British monarchy. In her lifetime, Queen Elizabeth took over 260 trips to more than 100 countries. On her official tours,

Queen Elizabeth with Nceba Faku, the then mayor of Port Elizabeth, South Africa in March 1995

US President George W. Bush with the Queen on the South Lawn of the White House, Washington, D.C., in May 2007

Queen Elizabeth's schedule was often very busy, with up to 10 official engagements every day. As well as meeting up with VIPs, Queen Elizabeth always tried to make time to greet the public in the countries that she visited.

The Royal Yacht *Britannia*

This elegant liner was the Royal Family's floating home during many official visits overseas. From 1953 until 1997, the Royal Yacht *Britannia* sailed over a million miles, carrying the Royal Family all over the world, including to many European countries, around the Caribbean, and several islands in the Pacific Ocean.

The Royal Yacht *Britannia* docked at Cape Town during Queen Elizabeth II's trip to South Africa in 1995.

Queen Elizabeth and her family also took holidays on *Britannia*, when the ship's crew organized games and treasure hunts for the children. The royal children had chores to do, too, such as cleaning the life rafts.

Queen Elizabeth on board *Britannia* in March 1972

Britannia is now docked in Edinburgh, Scotland, where it is open to the public.

Royal residences

Kensington Palace has been a royal residence since 1689. Queen Victoria was born there in 1819. Located in Kensington Gardens, it was the home of Prince William and his family until they moved to Windsor in 2022.

The palace gates are decorated with crowns, lions, and unicorns, which are symbols of the United Kingdom.

Kensington Palace in West London

Sandringham House in Norfolk

Sandringham is the royal residence near the Norfolk coast. It was Queen Elizabeth's favourite place to spend Christmas with her family.

The monarch's official Scottish home is the Palace of Holyroodhouse. Every year, Queen Elizabeth held a garden party there for 8,000 guests.

Holyroodhouse in Edinburgh

A love of horses

Queen Elizabeth had a lifelong passion for horses and ponies. She loved riding and going to the races. Queen Elizabeth owned her own stable of racehorses and always enjoyed watching them race – especially when they won!

Queen Elizabeth II at Newbury Racecourse in 2015

In 1976, her daughter, Princess Anne, competed in the equestrian events at the Olympic Games. Anne's daughter, Zara Phillips, won a equestrian team silver medal in the 2012 London Olympic Games. Princes William and Harry play polo, a game played on horseback.

Zara Phillips was the Individual Eventing World Champion in 2010. After her success at the London Olympics, she was part of the British team that won silver at the 2014 World Equestrian Games.

Royal Family tree

This family tree shows Queen Elizabeth's closest family members.

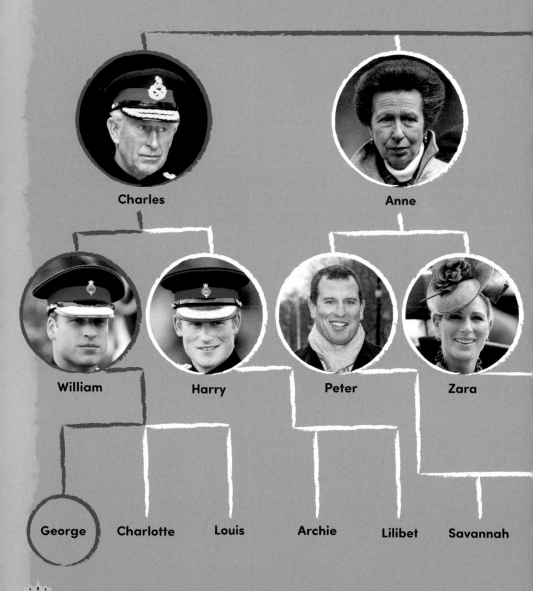

Charles

Anne

William

Harry

Peter

Zara

George

Charlotte

Louis

Archie

Lilibet

Savannah

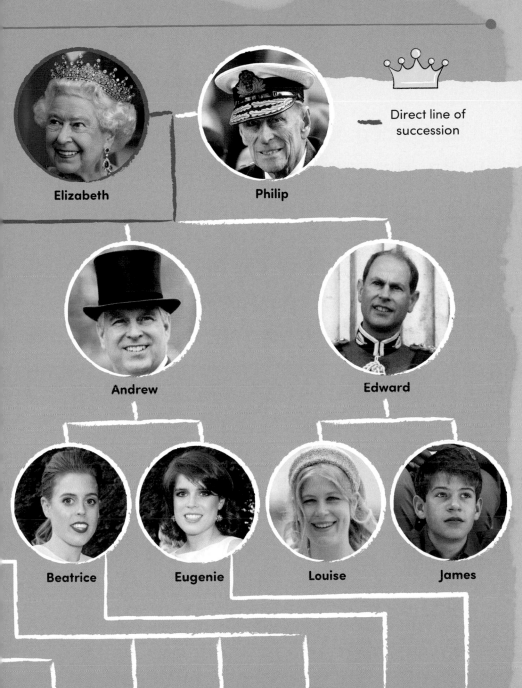

Elizabeth

Philip

Direct line of succession

Andrew

Edward

Beatrice

Eugenie

Louise

James

Isla

Mia

Lena

Lucas

Sienna

August

The Queen Mother

The Queen Mother was Queen Elizabeth's mum. She was born Elizabeth Bowes-Lyon and in 1923, she married Prince Albert. When he became King in 1936, taking the title of George VI, Elizabeth took on the role of Queen. She was a great support to her shy husband, and together they helped boost British morale during World War II.

After the King died and her daughter became Queen Elizabeth II, she took the title of Queen Mother.

The Queen Mother in 1954

On the Queen Mother's
90th birthday in 1990

The Queen Mother had a special bond with the British people. On her 100th birthday, huge crowds cheered her outside Buckingham Palace. She also received a telegram from her daughter to mark the occasion! The Queen Mother died in 2002 at the age of 101.

Prince Philip

When Princess Elizabeth married Philip Mountbatten in 1947, her father the King gave Philip the title His Royal Highness The Duke of Edinburgh.

Born in Greece, Philip was educated in England and became a British citizen. He was a Royal Navy officer when he married Elizabeth, but gave up his naval career to support her when she became queen. Queen Elizabeth and Prince Philip were married for 73 years, until his death in 2021 at the age of 99.

Elizabeth and Philip on their wedding day, 20 November 1947

Elizabeth and Philip renewed their wedding vows on their diamond anniversary, celebrating 60 years of marriage.

Prince Philip's major legacy is the Duke of Edinburgh's Awards. Since 1956, millions of young people have joined the scheme, which encourages activities such as physical fitness, volunteering, and outdoor expeditions. Since Prince Philip's death, the scheme has been led by his son Edward, Earl of Wessex.

Queen Elizabeth's children

Queen Elizabeth had four children. Charles was born in 1948. When he was 20 years old, he took the title of Prince of Wales. He has two sons, Princes William and Harry.

Prince Charles

Prince Charles with young people at the Oval, home of Surrey Cricket Club, in 2013

Anne, the Princess Royal, supports more than 300 charities and organisations. She competed in the 1976 Olympics as part of the equestrian team. Her children, Peter and Zara, do not have royal titles.

Princess Anne

Andrew, Duke of York, spent many years in the Royal Navy. His daughters are Princesses Beatrice and Eugenie.

Edward, Earl of Wessex, set up the Wessex Youth Trust with his wife, Sophie, to help young people. Their children are Lady Louise and James, Viscount Severn.

The Earl and Countess of Wessex with their children

William, Prince of Wales

Prince William and his mother, Diana, in 1991

Born in 1982, Prince William and his younger brother, Harry, grew up at Kensington Palace. They were both devastated when their mother, Diana, died in a car crash in France in 1997.

William first met his future wife, Catherine, when they were both students at the University of St Andrews in Scotland. After he graduated, William joined the RAF and became a search and rescue helicopter pilot.

William and Catherine married in 2011. They have three children – George, Charlotte, and Louis. Together, they lead the Royal Foundation of the Duke and Duchess of Cambridge, which mainly focuses on helping young people.

When William's father became King Charles III in 2022, he bestowed on his eldest son the title of Prince of Wales.

Football fan Prince William congratulates Jill Scott after England win the Women's Euro 2022 trophy.

Catherine, Princess of Wales

Catherine (Kate) Middleton met Prince William in 2001 at St Andrews University in Scotland, where she studied History of Art. After graduating, Kate worked for her family's online party goods business, and also for a fashion company.

After marrying William, Catherine threw herself into her new royal duties, becoming patron of

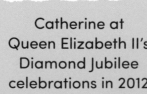

Catherine at Queen Elizabeth II's Diamond Jubilee celebrations in 2012

Catherine meets children in November 2015
as part of her work to promote good mental health.

more than 20 charities. She has said,
"I really hope I can make a difference,
even in the smallest way."

Catherine is a talented photographer,
and has taken many of the official
portraits of her three children, George,
Charlotte, and Louis.

A Royal Family wedding

Prince William and Catherine Middleton married on 29 April 2011, when Queen Elizabeth gave them the titles Duke and Duchess of Cambridge. More than 1,900 guests attended the wedding, and millions of royal fans watched the wedding on TV and online. The couple will one day become King William and Queen Catherine.

Prince George of Wales

Prince George, Queen Elizabeth's great-grandchild, was born in 2013. He is second in line to the throne after his father, the Prince of Wales. George's birth was

Prince George enjoys the Trooping the Colour ceremony with his father in 2015.

the first royal announcement by email. The news was also tweeted around the world – another first.

The prince has already taken on his share of offical duties. When he was just eight months old, baby George joined his parents on a royal visit to Australia

George heads home with his parents after his first royal tour to Australia in 2014.

and New Zealand. He has also visited Canada, Poland, and Germany with his parents and his sister, Charlotte.

Prince George and his father at the Platinum Jubilee in 2022

Princess Charlotte of Wales

When Princess Charlotte was born in 2015, she received many letters and cards of welcome, especially from girls named Charlotte! Some children also wrote to advise Prince George on how to be a good big brother.

Prince William and Catherine with Prince George and baby Princess Charlotte

Princess Charlotte in Norfolk on her seventh birthday, taken by her mother Catherine

Princess Charlotte Elizabeth Diana was named after her grandfather, King Charles III, her great-grandmother, Queen Elizabeth, and her grandmother Diana, Princess of Wales. She is third in line to the British throne, after her father and Prince George. She and her brothers go to the same school in Windsor.

Prince Louis of Wales

On 24 April 2018, cannons were fired and bells rang out to celebrate the birth of Prince Louis. He is the youngest child of Prince William and Princess Catherine and fourth in line to the British throne.

Louis was christened at St James's Palace in London. His parents followed royal tradition for the ceremony, including dressing the baby prince in a replica of the gown that

Catherine holds Prince Louis at his christening.

This portrait of Prince Louis was taken by his mother, Catherine.

Queen Victoria had made for her daughter's christening in 1841. The gown was made of lace lined with white satin.

In June 2022, Prince Louis attended his great-grandmother's Platinum Jubilee celebrations and stole the show, pulling lots of funny faces as he watched the colourful parades with his family.

Prince Harry, Duke of Sussex

Prince Harry was only 12 when his mother, Diana, died. In the days after their loss, Harry and William were looked after by their grandmother, Queen Elizabeth, at Balmoral Castle.

Harry served in the army for 10 years and completed two tours of Afghanistan.

Prince Harry with his regiment in Kandahar, Afghanistan, in 2009

The Duke and Duchess of Sussex with their children, Archie and Lilibet

In 2014, he set up the Invictus Games, a sports event for members of the military who have been injured in action.

Prince Harry married Meghan Markle in 2018. They have a son, Archie, and a daughter, Lilibet, named after Queen Elizabeth, whose family called her Lilibet. They live in the USA, with three dogs and some rescue chickens!

Royal celebrations

The year 2012 was extra special for Queen Elizabeth and the British people, with two major events to celebrate.

The first event was the Diamond Jubilee, when Queen Elizabeth became only the second British monarch, after Queen Victoria, to reign for 60 years.

At the Diamond Jubilee pageant, more than 1,000 boats sailed down the River Thames in London

All over the UK, people celebrated with street parties, picnics, and parades.

Later that summer, the Olympic Games were held in London. At the opening ceremony in the Olympic Stadium, the

James Bond, played by Daniel Craig, meets the Queen

audience watched film of the Queen meeting James Bond and getting into a helicopter with him.

Then a real helicopter hovered over the stadium – and the pair appeared to parachute into the arena! Of course, the parachutists were really stunt people, but the audience and everyone watching the ceremony on TV cheered and laughed.

The Platinum Jubilee

In June 2022, the UK took a four-day holiday to celebrate the Queen's 70-year reign. The fun began when thousands gathered in the Mall to watch a grand military parade. As well as picnics and street parties up and down the country, there was also a spectacular pageant telling the story of Queen's reign, and the Platinum Party – a huge music concert outside Buckingham Palace.

In Her Majesty's lifetime

Queen Elizabeth lived through a time of changes, both in Britain and across the world. Here are some of the most important events during her lifteime.

1926
Scottish inventor John Logie Baird invents the television.

1939
World War II begins, the biggest, most destructive war in history.

1948
The National Health Service is set up, providing free healthcare in the UK.

1928
In Britain, women over 21 are allowed to vote in elections.

1945
World War II ends in defeat for Germany.

1969
US astronaut Neil Armstrong is the first human to set foot on the Moon.

Neil Armstrong plants a US flag on the moon's surface.

Margaret Thatcher was UK prime minister for 11 years.

1973
The first-ever mobile phone conversation takes place in the USA.

1989
British scientist Tim Berners-Lee invents the World Wide Web.

2020
The COVID-19 pandemic means schools, offices, and shops close to help prevent the illness spreading.

1979
Britain elects its first woman prime minister, Margaret Thatcher.

2008
Barack Obama becomes the first-ever black US president.

2021
The first private flights into space begin, making space tourism possible.

The end of an era

In September 2022, just a few months after the joyful Platinum Jubilee celebrations, Her Majesty Queen Elizabeth II died, aged 96, at her beloved Balmoral Castle, in Scotland.

People in Britain and all over the world mourned the passing of Queen Elizabeth, but they also celebrated her devoted service to Britain, the

Queen Elizabeth's funeral was held at Westminster Abbey.

Commonwealth and the wider world. Before her funeral day, thousands of people queued for many hours to pay their last respects to their late Queen.

Green Park, near Buckingham Palace, was filled with tributes to the Queen.

The Queen's State Funeral was a huge event. In the UK alone, 28 million viewers followed it live on television. The streets were filled with crowds, and more than 2,500 military personnel took part in the moving funeral procession. The Queen's amazing life was over, but her legacy would live on forever.

The new King

After the death of his mother, Prince Charles became King Charles III. He could have chosen any of his four names – Charles Philip Arthur George. The King was not the only one whose title changed. His wife, Camilla, became the Queen Consort. The word "consort" is used for the partner of the monarch.

The new King and Queen Consort visit the Houses of Parliament to hear messages of support from MPs and Lords.

The new King greets mourners outside Buckingham Palace.

Although he became king as soon as his mother passed away, Charles was officially proclaimed monarch on 10 September 2022 at St James's Palace in London. For the first time, this ancient ceremony was shown live on television.

The proclamation was signed by the Privy Council. This group of special advisors to the monarch included UK prime minister Liz Truss, as well as six former British prime ministers.

A royal life story

This timeline shows all the personal landmarks in Queen Elizabeth's long, remarkable life.

1926
Princess Elizabeth is born.

1948
First son, Charles, is born.

1952
Elizabeth becomes Queen when King George VI dies.

1960
Second son Andrew is born.

1977
Silver Jubilee marks 25 years on the throne.

1950
Only daughter Anne is born.

1964
Youngest son Edward is born.

1982
Grandson William is born. He is second in line to the throne.

1947
Elizabeth marries Philip Mountbatten.

Queen Elizabeth cuts a cake commemorating her Platinum Jubilee in 2022.

2013
Great-grandson George is born. He is third in line to the throne.

2002
Golden Jubilee marks 50 years on the throne.

February 2022
Platinum Jubilee marks 70 years on the throne.

2017
Platinum wedding anniversary marks 70 years of marriage.

2012
Diamond Jubilee marks 60 years of Queen Elizabeth II on the throne.

September 2022
Queen Elizabeth II dies, aged 96.

2015
Queen Elizabeth becomes the longest serving British monarch.

2021
Prince Philip dies, aged 99.

Royal facts

In 1957, Queen Elizabeth became the first British monarch to broadcast their Christmas message on TV.

Queen Elizabeth celebrated two birthdays – her real one on 21 April, and the monarch's official birthday in June.

In her lifetime, Queen Elizabeth sat for more than 200 portraits, including a hologram.

The British Monarchy has an official website, YouTube channel, Twitter handle, Instagram account, and Facebook page.

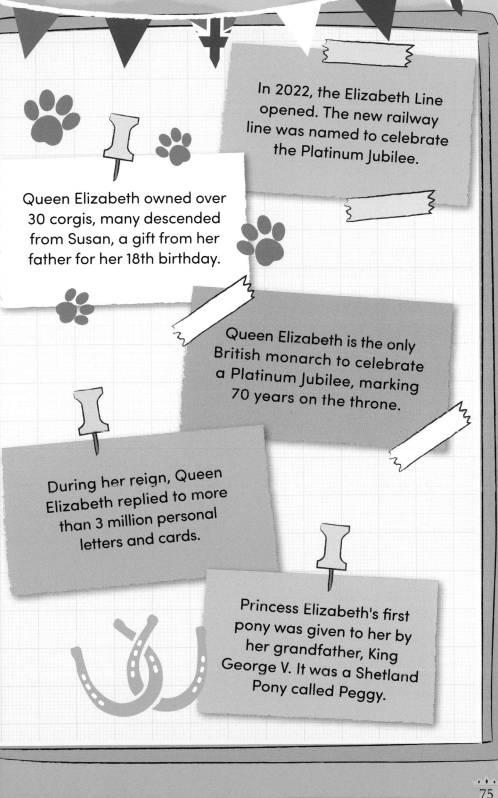

In 2022, the Elizabeth Line opened. The new railway line was named to celebrate the Platinum Jubilee.

Queen Elizabeth owned over 30 corgis, many descended from Susan, a gift from her father for her 18th birthday.

Queen Elizabeth is the only British monarch to celebrate a Platinum Jubilee, marking 70 years on the throne.

During her reign, Queen Elizabeth replied to more than 3 million personal letters and cards.

Princess Elizabeth's first pony was given to her by her grandfather, King George V. It was a Shetland Pony called Peggy.

Glossary

ancestor
family from
the past, such as
great-grandparents

coronation
official crowning
ceremony

head of state
highest or main
representative
of a country

legacy
an achievement
that lasts after
someone dies

monarch
king or queen

pageantry
grand display, often
of a ceremony

parliament
group of people
who make the laws
in a country

royal regalia
symbols of royalty,
such as a crown
and sceptre

reign
time during which
a monarch is on
the throne

residence
home